EVERYONE KNOWS I AM A HAUNTING

ACKNOWLEDGEMENTS

Thank you to my brothers and my grandmothers.

This book would not be tangible without the discernment and guidance of my publisher, Jeremy Poynting of Peepal Tree Press, or the indefatigable work of his deputy, Hannah Bannister.

I've attended workshops administered by Merle Hodge and Funso Aiyejina (Cropper Foundation Residential Workshop for Writers, 2010), Monique Roffey (St. James Writers' Room, 2014), and Gregory Pardlo (Callaloo Creative Writing Workshop, 2016). I've benefited from the critical insight and creative fellowship I received there, from both my instructors and fellow participants.

Thank you to Danielle Boodoo-Fortuné, who is both sister and poem.

I'm grateful for the attentions and cares of Marina Salandy-Brown and Joan Dayal, who have supported my work with unfailing generosity.

Thank you to Olive Senior, Rajiv Mohabir, Loretta Collins Klobah, Vahni Capildeo, Ayanna Gillian Lloyd, Andre Bagoo, Mark Ramsay, elisha efua bartels, Lisa Allen-Agostini, Colin Robinson, Alake Pilgrim, Sharon Millar, Marielle Forbes, Almah LaVon Rice, and Anu Lakhan, I am humbled by your individual and collective regard.

I am moved by the visual articulation of Mark Jason Weston and Kriston Chen in designating a cover that speaks so urgently to my work.

I have been guided by outstanding educators in Literatures in English, and I am more thankful than I can say for the tutelage of Carol Montserin and the late Giselle Rampaul.

This book of poems would not have been published without the strange and certain counsel of Nicholas Laughlin.

Finally, thank you to McKinley Hellenes Krantz, for whom and in whom these poems find home.

My gratitude to the editors of the following journals, who first published versions of these poems: *Alice Yard*, *The Asian American Literary Review*, *The Caribbean Review of Books*, *Cordite Poetry Review*, *Moko Magazine*, *Small Axe*, *Susumba's Book Bag*, *tongues of the ocean*.

EVERYONE KNOWS I AM A HAUNTING

SHIVANEE RAMLOCHAN

PEEPAL TREE

First published in Great Britain in 2017
Peepal Tree Press Ltd
17 King's Avenue
Leeds LS6 1QS
UK

ISBN 13: 9781845233631

Supported using public funding by
ARTS COUNCIL
ENGLAND

CONTENTS

I

II: The Red Thread Cycle

III

For my mother, Deborah,

and my father, Suresh

I

A NURSERY OF GODS FOR MY HALF-WHITE CHILD

Ganesh
means some names come before even your mother's;
means a trunk is the hipswell of a banyan,
and the thickest root of a beast;
means a trumpet in your palm, gold
and glistening before it meets your lung-alarums;
means a round belly will roll you over hard times,
your navel pointing upward to your heart.

Kali says
– Black is not a bastard skin tone.
The first woman boiled black in an eldritch kitchen;
lay it out on the thin back of the world for the sun's grave.
– If you must cry for a man, do it dancing on his skull.

Shiva means don't shoot what you can devour.

Krishna vaults in your cradle,
summoning gopis with pails of milk.
When you count, Saraswati threads
an abacus of air and dreaming
into the plushness of your palms.

One day, when I am the one who turns to you for feeding
you will spoon the names of these gods over my false teeth.
You will soak them into my palate, remind me
there is no such thing as an accidental shrine.

One day, when I am so close to dying that my shadow
splits off at the ankles,
runs down to the bush ponds to escape the flesh decay –
drown me to sleep with the names of the gods you have made

shrieking, floating, bastarding into birth,
called to the world of the living between the harvest of your thighs.

TO LIVE IN THE NEW YEAR

My new husband is a thaumaturgist.
Tenderly, he plants songs in me,
the better to treat the new year
with fire.

This, for charity, he utters,
melting frozen lappe marrow on my thighs.
Last night, while he dreamt, the Northern Range lovered me,
kissed me unkind, watched me
break my fifth and sixth ribs on the Blanchisseuse rocks.

A shattered staghorn coral blade sinks between my vertebrae,
seaweed-shone, saltproofed & undrowning in my red matter.

While he sleeps, I check on my old wife in the stables.
I watch her bridling our beasts.
Lightning triple-mounts the sky, crests firecracker angry in straw snaps.
Tiny pellets of ruin scatter our horses.
The other animals, yet unnamed,
hiss and flicker out under the stars.

She summons the menagerie with dried game.
Sandpaper tongues rasp damp meat from her knuckles. She pulls
the dying stem from my body, sinks that coral into her mouth.
Together, we sit and watch fields glow umber.
The island startles into her first, final days.

THE ABORTIONIST'S DAUGHTER
DECLARES HER LOVE

Here is the church. These are the doors that open to the sea.
My grandmother once knelt here, awed, a special guest to an exorcism.

It is nothing like the movies would have you think,
she told me, and I believed her.

They have called me many things between these aisles,
she told me, and I believed her.

That is the trouble with our trade, she said.
When men aspire to terrible jobs, we offer them hushed respect,
the blushing necks of virgins.
Women wearing the same gloves, sorting the same straight-backed pins
between the prayers of their teeth,
are taught to deserve nothing more than an acreage of sorrow.

Why an acreage?
Never give a woman more sadness than she needs.
From this fabric, from this persistent earth, she will wrangle
greater things than men can fathom.
She will wrestle squalling tar infants from the mire, and those children
shall stumble upwards, slicing through the spines of men
who have offended their mothers.

Give a woman an acreage of humiliation, with one spade,
one crucifix, one box of straight-backed pins.
You've given her nothing she can grow.
Within the year she will run up hard against the borders of her land,
shrieking, scouring the air for a way to flee her sex.

Give her enough land to hang herself.

Here is the church. It lies close to the land that they gave us.
Come see the land of my grandmother, and her mother, and hers.
Come walk on the borders of my mother's land, where no trees grow.

THE ABORTIONIST'S DAUGHTER
GIVES COLD COMFORT

Careful.
Your tears will thin these good stitches.

Here is a sadder story, to damp this moment's scar.

The girl came to us near nude, defiance
limning her jaw, a coven of welts
witching dark spells around her waist.
Do me, she told us, ankles thudding on
the metal table. Take it out.

But there are some places our knives dare not go.
The law would lash us to the trees,
pitch forest fires from the roots of our hair,
scalpel through
and through us.

She howled. She cursed the clinic
from bedrock quartz to pitch-pine rafter.
She christened my gloves with shame. These utensils
have never recovered. Here her ghost resides,
shrieking
as we part the thighs of young girls.

She scours their insides for surrogate hope.

How she died is another day's work.

MY SISTER OF THE CORAL MOUTH

Forgive me.

I was instructed not to pray for you,
daughter who drowned her wrong child
at our ocean's worst fault.

Furrowed soil and scapulae lie at cross purposes in a sea cavern.
No one could knit it but
you.
At night, when all else fails to remember my name,
I hear you,
sewing drought in damp recesses,
reckoning your sins in sargasso thread.

Counting
reaving
cleaving at your breastbone
with that wet star of your dead son's clavicle,
whittled to fine whiteness.

The man who got that infant on you glowers in our marketplace.
You hollow him with the ghosts you've made.
The haunting
steals chunks of his liver; the grief grinds him shorter
in each dry season's dust.

Soon he will stand at the height he forced you, on your stitcher's knees.

I carry your son's name under my tongue in barbed suture.
You wanted my speech to keep his first memory safe.

On that fault line,
beneath the archipelagic eyelid of the cavern you grew,

you test yourself with sharp filial bones,
writhing. Ghosting the bedrock.
Waiting in the sudden wail.

DUENNE LILITH

Mother
scalds each window from our house, unhinges
Father
by the jaw so he may never sing you closer.

He breaks, weeping, but
I basket his falling ribs
like you did, before the woods
called you to bride.

Your forest is named for cuts.

Sister,
find me. Pierce
the wasp-netting that masks me, sternum to swollen lids
with your goddess tongue. Haunt me; say
my name and hoard me – fold my bones, fit me thimbled, docile –
I will breathe into the welts, endure it.

Save me.

For you, I wear this crucible hatchery of cocoyea broom bruises.
For you, I kissed into each lash, denying your death,
crying against the devil's spit on your mandible,
her scorpion peppers melting into the carriage
of your straw hat.

Tonight
I press our father's body back together. I watch him limp
towards his marriage bed.

Sister, keep vigil.
Our eyeless homestead remembers your touch. Tonight,
the galvanize rattles a Holi hymn, waiting,

rust-pealing a dread lovesong to the sound of your
heels,
backwards-skirting in the dirt yard.

DUENNE LARA

If
I write into you hard enough
the rumour murmurs that you'll come for me.

If
I scratch you through the water mirror, suck you under my talons,
will you knock & claim me? I keep
this one soft garden in my trachea vacant; I
stripped speech for split gourds, choking on seeds so you
might come live in me, little
lover, come
claim these metatarsal prayers.

Everyone knows I am a haunting.

Enact it again, you whisper, using mora and purpleheart to tell me.
Mourn me all over, cloister to caul.
Weep me upright in our wedding bower, my little bride, and I
do, I do,

I take the four rivers of the forest by throat and algal sinew,
pump the waters into my lungs. Come,
I'll christen you away from the devil's doorstep,
duenne suitor, duenne saviour, duenne dowry,
Duenne, you are mine

by sharp incense and pistol recoil, by moth fabric and mouth to mouth.
The wooden atlas delivers deeper rings in us
while the devil tries again to win your heart,
grinning.

Come here, she marrow-bites.
I have something for you, but it looks like torture.
She scrapes it from the ruins of the moonlight museum.
She smiles as it eats our national anthem from your tongue.

No one told you how it would hurt, to have your feet forced against
family hearth.
The mangroves stroked you taut while the devil cracked your bones right,
a blister body of devotion
a casket of cunning charms to stamp you for her service.

I will never make you walk again, if you will be mine.

DUENNE LORCA

Darling son, the dark is here. Take your father's bois and skirt
to the eyelid of forest edge.

On the day you were born, I didn't bless you.
I damped my dress with your purplish blood and rinsed you in the river,
stained my mouth
with the placenta of your leavings.
You were my first child, and my best.

Darkling son, neither female nor filial,
the schoolmistress tried to beat the unchristian out of you.
I rinsed her religion from your blue shirt every Sunday.
I kept your khakis clean and my own tail hidden.

Nothing the forest raises is a monster.
Your sisters, red howler and river otter,
renounced school for the kiss of brushbroom-altar,
water sweetening their pelts.
Your father hid their navel strings in El Cerro del Aripo;
lock by lock they build the hairbeds for their own children's haunts.

Teeth-grit your father's bois and climb.
Though knuckles bruise and your ankles snap southward, climb.
Though rivers flow against their hearts and I cannot follow you upward,
climb.

Dreadling son, I am but one mother, tail and all.
Tell your sisters I am sorry.
Tell the woods you will make a faithful bride.

Take your own feet as dowry.
Turn a poem under Spanish tongue for each green ladder you breach
into your husband, the mountain's back.
Trust no one with your straw hat.

I SEE THAT LILITH HATH BEEN WITH THEE AGAIN

Love,
I saw our daughter in the grocery store again.
This time, she'd discarded the old shoes,
because finally,
her hooves are coming through.

She was using her talons to tear through meat packets.

Oh, honey, I frowned.
Your mum is a vegan.
Our daughter followed me to the produce aisle, and she chewed
one carrot, sadly, to try to make me happy. It didn't take.

She could barely tame the wild things of her teeth.

We sat and talked in the trunk of my car for about
fifteen minutes afterwards. I offered to pay for her shopping.
She said,

Mother, don't bother. I'm covered. I've got it
sorted, between the furnace and the fire and
the pit of my stomach does all my flame charring anyway. I'm
set, for days.

She said, "Tell Mum don't worry. I've got a nice place. No boys.
I'm finishing up my degree and I don't dream of having fathers;
not anymore. You raised me well, you can't even tell
where the roots of my hair
used to be."

She said, "I'm sorry I didn't want the same life as you both did."
I guess that's what most mothers want to hear.

Honey, oh honey,
we did good.

Lilith sends us love and photographs of her last kill.
We made a mantelpiece of her baby antlers. We know
how to breathe now, how not to be
ungrateful. We love her; we just
don't want the same things she did.
That's all.

THE VIRGIN SPEAKS OF WHAT SHE ENDURED

Don't turn the lamps down.

The mangrove burned for days. When our forest gave up her bare shoulders to the hungry women and children, for weeks, we ate nothing but trees.

In the first week, the vines, the shoots, the leaves helped us make soup.

In the second week we crammed roots through the holes in our teeth.

In the third week, my sister's hair fled her blue scalp; in the fourth week my sister trapped and gnawed a blue crab to death with no fire but her belly.

By the fifth week the bruised bark had nothing left, so we began to eat language.

On the sixth week I dreamed an ocelot brought me your name in the cradle of his tongue.

There was no seventh week of which I can speak, and on the dawning of the eighth week,

you and the battalion returned.

You've told me of how the war crumbled cathedrals of bamboo and stone before your eyes. There are great, open plains where the high streets shone. The statues of the men who spoonfed us English are ground to glassine.

I am no longer your bride. We ate the words for marriage, for sacrament, for lawfully wed. I fed my sister the ivory dress, so she might keep warm; I placed the pearlseed buttons where her eyes once shone.

Don't turn the lamps down. Look at me, the price of revolution.
I left the fighting words alive for tonight. I didn't eat triumph,
or victory, or maidenhead.

Starving, I unswallowed the words that mattered.

Look here, the glassine road of our crushed forefathers wraps around my belly. Our eyes are now the only mirrors, fusilier of mine.

My surgeon. My soldier.
My small, bare breasts sit as quiet as mute brown doves.
Show me why I waited.

Come, burst me into song.

MATERNA

I am not your mother.
Where she is, an isthmus hence,
salt trees whisper your name to her.
If she plugs her ears, the sound will find her;
if she runs to church
to plead true shrift
your face will unblot itself in years of
Hail Marys, prayers that come apart
in her hands
as she clasps them.
Her old prayers quiver, faced with fresh ghosts.

I am not your mother.
Where she died, a tree grew, swearing as it
twisted roots through her bones.
No tree loves to lie with a thief.
Some say she sleeps beneath silk cotton, but
that would be too perfect a fate.
Let her struggle each night in a
mangrove thicket; let her wince at the
deforester's blade on her back,
probing,
testing three canals filled with raw hurt.

I am not your mother.
No one in this world can love that girl like her mother,
they told me, the day
I tore out my hair to hold you.
My hair, the raft lashed with pitch darts that kept you.
My hair, the mantle against
less honourable creatures who blow
kisses with crusted lips.
They measure you for marvellous coffins.
My dead hair was never your shroud.

My hair is the hundred thousand wires
of my love and it holds you safe.
In its jungle, you are queen.
In it, you learned that ink and blood,
and salt, that these three grow
the truest trees.

I am not your mother,
but in my womb there is the knowing of you.
The dome of my head is shorn close, 'til it hints of marrow.
These years and years of hair
carpet your dreams.

FIRE, FIRE

Outside the tent, it is very cold. I am from islands; I think he doesn't
know what my skin can endure. But I see I have misjudged
him; inside the tent I am bivouacked by poems; he is no great orator
but they keep me warm. Who told you these tales, I ask him as he
whispers fire, fire on my breastbone. I show him where the war took
most of me; we agree the hole can never be filled.

When he does not pretend that we can transplant a sapling in the space
where my family died, then I begin to love him.

Fire, fire
he soothes into my brow. His grandmother was the one to feed him these
poems, and to keep my red skin warm he shares her battle stories. He tells
me about the canyons beneath her beaded blouses; he recites her own
poems about the times she was held down. Oh,
fire, fire
sets the leather shell of our tent alight; the truth is
too hot to hold and all I want is to be burned.

It gets so cold that the rivers forget how to dream in thaw tongues; it
gets so cold, the ice grows everywhere except on his grandmother's
poems. Giving me her language, he keeps none for himself. I love him
and now I must watch him freeze to death.

Fire, fire
I try to skitter across his blue cheeks, but those
wedding vows do not dissolve in my spit; some poems are not
transferrable. This heat,
this love, is a terrible gift.

THE ABORTIONIST'S GRANDDAUGHTER
GIVES BLOOD

I do what I can do. I hold him close.
His limbs are antler-heavy, his torso the belly of a stag
split to reveal giant crags of ice, glistening with
a warning. I'm desperate. I have no good poems about fire.

I shake him. I stutter.
These are my grandmother's poems, these, now,
are all I can offer.
Rocking him in my burning arms, I feed him.

Blood, blood.
I am the daughter of women who knew surgical guilt,
stitchery, straight-backed pins and swollen udders. I am
the daughter of abortionists, I
feed my husband
blood, blood
and our tent chokes on the startled heat of two bodies
blistering naked onto new pages,
gasping, learning
how to breathe,
how to survive with
so much fire.

KISKADEE BRIDE

In the courtyard, all our throats are burst figs.
Each cry is its own tyrant.

Beaks mark the pulse of entrail-love, cooing in yellowflesh.

Call your husband passerine,
feel him flit a goodbye beneath your eyelash.

Call your husband shrike,
sound your mourning bellow in the bill of his last farewell.

Call your husband home,
watch wings strum the hurricane screen,
wet like November in Lopinot,
wetter than a split-throat struck talon-hard from above.

In the courtyard at night, close your eyes.

Be yourself braceleted in cagewire.
Be feasted upon by greedy mouth, by guttural swoop.

Hold his small prey in your open heart,
let the whole flock eat you out of the small rooms where you wait
to be made into a triplenotched perch.

Where all his cries in your cleft throat echo yes,
echo bright,
echo

kiss-kill me, kiss-kill me, kiss-kill me,

carry him home to the cauldron of your canary bed.

CARACARA

Your husband takes the bird home when you falter. He does not strip
the body bare.
You return from the hunt to find it lain in the middle of your marriage bed.
Over fourteen days the flesh rots into cereus, chokes the bower
with bloom.

Then comes the stripping. The dismantling of muscle makes you sick,
sends you scalding
out your womb with harpsichord and harmonium – his grandfather's
music, and yours.
Anything to keep the density of cartography from the sheets.

I cannot bear it, you tell him. You watch him whittle, solving for
pressed feathers,
sucking math from the broken truss. The bird's cold throat, red crest,
the bird's ribs
splitting, salt marrow spread under your man's gums.

I cannot, you say, spitting him clean and starting over.
Still, the bird keeps on giving.

Your husband threads each splintered process into sharp jewellery,
hooks the bone spurs
in your lobes for temple.
Dead as alive, devoured whole.
                              He picks your teeth clean whilst he prays,
your shy falconer, hunting in the night, holding mass
for his friend in the flowers.

II

THE RED THREAD CYCLE

1. On the Third Anniversary of the Rape

Don't say Tunapuna Police Station.
Say you found yourself in the cave of a minotaur, not
knowing how you got there, with a lap of red thread.
Don't say forced anal entry.
Say you learned that some flowers bloom and die
at night. Say you remember stamen, filament,
cross-pollination, say that hummingbirds are

vital to the process.

Give the minotaur time to write in the police ledger. Lap
the red thread
around the hummingbird vase.

Don't say I took out the garbage alone and he grabbed me by the waist
and he was handsome.
                Say Shakespeare. Recite Macbeth for the tropics.
Lady Macbeth was the Queen of Carnival
and she stabbed Banquo with a vagrant's shiv during J'ouvert.
She danced a blood dingolay and gave her husband a Dimanche Gras
upbraiding.

I am in mud and glitter so far steeped that going back is not an option.
Don't say rapist.

Say engineer of aerosol deodorant because pepper spray is illegal,
anything is illegal
Fight back too hard, and it's illegal,
>your nails are illegal

Don't say you have a vagina, say
he stole your insurance policy/ your bank boxes/ your first car
downpayment

Say
he took something he'll be punished for taking,
not something you're punished for holding
like red thread between your thighs.

II. Nail It to the Barn Door Where It Happened.

This is how you survive it.
When the doctor stitching the torn seam of your sex
pauses to tend a text message,
spit on him.

Learn to drive, just so
you can take yourself to Galera Point.
Stand closer to the edge of the land than you ever have.
Feel the spray lick your one ruined ankle.
You must carry out the unspeakable thing you came here to do.
Do it well.
Leave the tools of your doing to line the brush path back, like a trail
of blackened flambeaux bottles.

When you get back home, take your mother down from the mantelpiece,
and tell her the unspeakable thing.

I have to mention that it will hurt.
I have to mention that it may not cure.

Go to the movies all alone, to the last show that's
showing on its last day, so no one but you will be there.
Even so, the floors will be sticky.
Make love to yourself in the darkness, in any way you can bear it.
You will be sticky, departing.
Grin, even so.

Use your mother's scissors to cut out the words
[father] [minister] [boyfriend] [wife]
Pick the right word, and nail it to the barn door
where it happened.
Take aim. Don't tell me what weapon.

Shatter the wood, saying,
"You did not break me.
You did not break me.
Yesterday, I learned to walk again."

Your ankle will still be ruined forever.
Blast the bolted doors into hell's abattoir.

III. You Wait for Five Years, and Then

After,
you think of walking. You
want to take one step farther
than the riptide that nearly drowned you in 98.

You were eleven, then, knowing nothing
about first blood, of what the moon would write
on your belly.

What language might barbwire a bare flank. How,
yes, you can sew protection in this space,
here,
a palm span beneath the thing he did, to begin it.

You take no one's counsel. Head for the
earth that might have you. Hollow a pit that breathes,
gives pain, does not swallow. The night watches.
You are turning in, tuning deeper,
battering out a girl that reckons victories
in pockets of white stones.

You lick each pebble clear of littoral salt.
Every one's a blinded fish eye. They hoard up your pockets,
and you wait for it to happen again.

The first year sees you gallop.
The second year finds you shattering crutches.
The third year loves the shine in your teeth while you choose
for the first time, in a cane field.
The fourth year flows in forty rivers and lesser tributaries,
from the banks of the Caroni River where the body will be cremated
according to Hindu rites.

The fifth year watches you forget your fisheye stones
on the breast of the lover you chose.

You walk into the market, undefended.
Nothing drowns you, when you see him again. Nothing comes to swallow.
The murder you said you would make sinks,
a dead gaze of blanched ore. You watch him grin,
remembering.

IV: The Policeman in Your Throat

The policeman bids you closer. His gun is a live witness; you can't tell
how hard it's breathing until he has you by the larynx, and you are
howling
[murder] [horror] [I know your daughter]
but he has snapped your vocal cords for stubborn weeds
and put them to bed.

You are in the Caroni Savannah.
You are praying for traffic, for the grace of headlights
unstitching the dark, for just one farmer to corrupt the quiet,
to tractor country warnings and cutlass luck.

The policeman's boot blesses the small of your back. You are
still praying, but these are new psalms,
and they have no likeness in holy writ.

This is not the poem you said you would write, but there is nothing
for it.

There is only the policeman, rum bristle, handcuff come, ledger
welt,
reading you your rights. He pitches you open,
haunts your swallow, grinds the psaltery of
this small song, this only ode you find you still know.

The policeman smashes the lyre you were,
and there is tall grass to veil you,
there are no farmers to raise you,
no one comes to blot you up from this novitiate earth
where you're buried now.

V: The Five Count

The first time they try it on you, it's Holi.
The sun is something precious on the back of your neck.
It's the first time you have an ochre nape.
You watch the cape of your breathing pitch spit stones over the
temple tiles.

The second time, you know what to call it.
You have a whistle; you're not so foolish that you don't know what
to blow down on when things like this come knocking.
No one's cut the grass at the community centre for seven months,
and you have razor shins you can't explain to your grandmother.

I fell, you say. I keep falling.

She prays for oxblood, for all we don't feed to skinny boys. She
makes of it a song, a clot of chewed cane, a cutlass you keep when
she burns into the Caroni.

The third time he tries it on you, his throat makes a sound like
dying beetles in the dry season.
Sorry. It's the acid reflux, baby.
You put your fists up, wrists out.
You swallow a black beetle and it tastes
like powder, pressed in clay.

There is cold sweat.
There are ashes that circle in beer; there is his ceiling
and now you know the beams of it.

The fourth time is the fourth time. A man's spine is a slick rosary.
A man's heart is a cushion for the cutlass you never use.
You are a pretty boy. You are not poor,
and you have both your knees.

The fifth time, ocean. The saltwater of the fifth time sucks blue beads
off the broken dais
of both palms. There is so much fifth time. Stop now.
Fifth time I'm begging,
fifth heartbeat like a fight soundtrack, swallow your fifth as though
it were your own small fist pumped back into your belly,
a sudden score of fifths falling off the regatta, smashing its wet heart
against the rigging of your sternum.

It is time to stop counting.

VI: Public Holiday.

I am working to train the flinch out of myself.
The rapist helped; it was Whitsunday, it was Kartik.
I remember something holy being leavened between bodies,
I remember bread. This is an oven; this is how you hide in it.

I recall the sugar-press of his mouth on my nape,
and the prayer of thanks. I recall that it was my thanks, shorn as
offering.
He said, you may not thank me now, bird bones. You may not praise the
welts.
It was Nauratum; it was Monday Mass.
His breath was molasses. He chewed my spine, snapped cervical
wires, suckling
marrow and electricity under his sweet tongue.

I tasted my own praise in the press of his mouth. This is a heat song,
he swore, sinking that kiss into the day that was
Imbolc, it was Dassera. I remember something wet
being blotted over ankles. I remember the ocean,
the immersion of a man.
His clean shoulders disappeared into the drink, steady with my neck
in his molars, ground down to pink dust and spit.

If it was Divali, don't tell me about it. I am working to steady the hair
trigger, to still my pulse and to check for vital signs.
The rapist helped. This is how you say it, he sung, chording the rifle
with my vertebrae, cocking the bass line on his lungs.

Say, thank you for this hurt that will feed your best verse.
Say thank you. Say it.
I sang soft praise, blessing the night, and it was a moveable feast,
circling the wrist of every good girl,
called to the table of what rises, bread blistering the teeth.

VII: The Open Mic of Every Deya, Burning.

I took to that stage knifed in,
leaking witch hazel and chandelier bush, briar-packed by puncheon
hard enough to fuck that three-day sickness to the cross.

I ground the belly of my gun against his bare flank,
against his sour stem still dripping with me.

When the poem told me to go on my knees, I went.

I limped past high road through the dry river gutter, my love.
I let the glass pauper my shins.
I lit hurricane lamps with the lucifers of the stake he splintered
six inches inside me, six
knuckle-fathoms deep.

The poem says
truss him gullet to groin with leather and lyre-wire.
Loop the cry around your wrist
like he wound your hair to the bedpost and knotted you there
for safe keeping.

The poem says, "Give no thanks."

I tell it,
flinching through the verses, fumbling for a post to push me upright.
I strip, feel spectator eyes finger the crumbled spires where my wings
used to be.

There lies an ache
in the place I was ransacked. Only this poem knows it.
Each line break bursts me open
for applause, hands slapping like something hard and holy
is grating out gold halleluiahs
beneath the proscenium of his grave.

III

ALL THE DEAD, ALL THE LIVING

At Jouvay, it eh matter if you play yourself
or somebody else.

Play your dead eighty-year-old granny,
who had tongue like scorpion pepper,
two foot like twinned fishtail in Caura River,
a smile like a butterknife cutting through hot sada.

Play your living mother,
who made of more parts glitter than flour,
who teach you softness have more than enough space
to leave a cutlass waiting,
glistening between fat folds,
ready to chop yuh from a bed of ample waist.

Play all the dead and all the living in you,
in yuh shortpants,
in yuh badjohn drawers,
in yuh ragged fishnets and curry-gold battyriders,
in yuh half-top, in yuh no-top,
breasts swinging under electric-tape nipples,
panty forgotten in a culvert overflowing with holy water and hell liquor,
your own perspiration sliding between bodies at play
like the wetness from your body is purgatory-unction.

Play yuhself.
Clay yuhself.
Wine en pointe and wine to the four stations of the cross,
dutty angel,
bragadang badting,
St. James soucouyant,
deep bush douen come to town
to make a killing in mud and mudder-in-law
on fresh doubles, after.

Play like you eh playing in your public servant office on Ash Wednesday,
calves aching and twitching in sensible slingback heels,
a pulse in your lower back blossoming
each time you bend down to file a papers,
salute a clerk,
say grace before ashes.

You know where you are, really.
Just how you know the clerk is a chantwell,
the office is a concrete antechamber before the final mas,
the pavement is a busshead-convergence,
the parking lot is a gayelle,
the savannah is a arena where paint and abeer might wash,
but spirit does linger.

You eh waiting til next year.
Where you plant yourself this Jouvay
is where your spectral, midnight lagahoo rattling she coffin,
turning wolf
to woman
to wolf again.

CATCHING DEVI & SHAKUNTALA

Pull the girl out of that body tonight.

Be her grandmother, sifting flour through fingernails,
swelling roti like bruises under skin.
Be her mother, bound for Brasso with a cocoa pod
wet under her book of bhajans.

Be the daughter that rises from her,
shortskirted and fullflamed
improbable & darkskinned
like wet mango leaves slick with puja oil in your palms.

In a house on a hill giving birth to the sea,
all your daughters are waiting.
In the arms of the mangrove snaking under Mosquito Creek,
all your mothers are braiding.

In the kajal your grandmother wept out before her wedding,
In the kalsa spilling over,
in the bower of that Barrackpore night

in your daughter's darkmouth on her lover,
their hair in oiled snakes weeping bright,
bindis licked askew and limping over kisscured skin,
pleading

to pull every girl out of every body tonight
to ransom every woman from the three canal
to cure every remedy in a ruined field
to tell your daughters to run, run,

kiss,

flee.

SHEPHERDESS BOXCUTTER: ONE

Shepherdess Boxcutter,
I drove the north coast road for you. I saw women pull portents
from the shore,
obeah them whole, salt them down and take them home, but you
were nowhere.
A red flag chipped my tooth.
A red wave went from the pillar of my heart to the archery of my cunt.

I kept you everywhere but safe. I hoisted that flag into the sea,
scooped our son out and dried him,
dangled turtleskull and tamarind knots over his sternum to keep
him safe by night.

We invent the beasts that we breed.
We silence the night with the startle of our starvers.
So salve me.
Seek me in the ruins of that old cave, find me flinging

red flags over eye and under fist to say what I haven't said, to let
the pitch bind me.
Blind me.
Dredge me up from the wet rocks, salt me with something good,
take me home to our mother, who knows best how we are wed.

SHEPHERDESS BOXCUTTER: TWO

Shepherdess Boxcutter, this is how you open your mouth.

At seventeen I learned how to choke the rape out,
how to guard my house with small arms of casing,
shells wet with grave rain.
The abacus of my bonework kept the hearth lit.

I lost an arm in the building of my house, and the morass claimed it.
Scout to the farthest split lip of the coast where I grew.
Dredge it out of the water.
Bring me home and watch me shake hands with my first hammer.

Listen. I've needed other men, not you. I've breathed with other beasts,
and called it clemency,
called it first communion, called it a gayelle full of buss mouth
on nights when your bois drops to the level of your split knuckles.

No one but you knows where my arm is buried.

I don't want to buss your mouth.
I want to bless it.
Come closer. Come coastal on the unbruised lip between here,
hereafter,
and the cutlass line of your last lover.

Come open your mouth.

NO CURANDERA BUT YO SÓLA

María swallowed my knucklebone one minute after being born. You
heard the scream but kept silent.
I have written short letters ever thereafter,
thanking la virgen sagrada,
thanking the thrashtongued goddess of my own shrine,
the short door of straining birth,
the oil on my forehead,
the sweat of small fantasmas growing our daughter her teeth.

María en la playa sorting which shells to drown.
María en el campo playing resurrection with the butcher's girl.
María's eyes, when you explain
reliquaria | sacrificio | soucouyant

María, I tell her, gathering sargassum y red chaparral,
before I met your father my whole life was backcountry.
Our first kiss was a hinterland; in it he learned
there are more rivers on an island than he knew,
that the sun can set in a torn thread of sarisilk,
that Divali noche is blacker than las olas del mar, judging him,
sealashing him out of a safer life.

My daughter in the ruined arms of a fairground Shiva, sticking
his blue plaster with the aum thrice-etched in her orhni.
My daughter the bishop, blessing a lesser child's head in the fields,
crumbling paste on his flaxbrow.
My daughter at Holi, mistaking abeer for blood,
drinking all the same,
drinking, wild and different,
drinking with my knuckle in the warning of her jaw.

SONG OF THE ONLY SURVIVING GRANDMOTHER

The wind that midwifed you
was unafraid to be curry-thick.

Aji, I believe
I hear your bootfall in my dreams.

While I sleep,
you cut through cane.

You wash the baby-work from your legs
and turn back to the farm.

Three sons, and a daughter.
Three stillbirths,
and three sons again.

You teach me to be sad,
but to be sad and work.

Pull the calf loose while your heart breaks.
Scythe the tall grass and take another drink.
Stoke the fire.
Soak in puncheon.
Your grief is a broken calf you cannot outrun.

The world can't end when there are your animals left to feed,
when your man writhes in the stables, drunk,
in need of milking 'til he's dry-eyed
and bawling, *Ganesh!*
Ganesh!
His nose pressed udder-deep in cow breast.

At night, thirty years before I get born,
your lost children whistle through gaps in the farm floor,
culling up from the earth,
ghost-limbs swelling from mapepire snakebite.

GOOD NAMES FOR THREE CHILDREN

Do not go into the dark alone.
Hold my hand; I don't care if it
embarrasses you, or makes you fret,
squirm like you were trying to crawl out
of your own skin.
You pull away and slice me across
my Achilles' heels.
Three years later you will fling yourself from me
into the grinning gamble of oncoming traffic
and your years of being carried
will rush up like starving orphans to kiss your palms.
Do not go into the dark alone.

Remember your right to use it –
your voice, your arms, your
High Street San Fernando desire for the
girl with an orange blossom tucked behind her ear.
Do not wake, sleep-ransacked,
bleary-eyed with a fraud's tears,
feeling filthy for the way you love,
the how, the who, the where.
I cradled your strong limbs in my belly
and they tapped out against my bones
the morse code of your whole life.
Remember your right to use it.

Do not forget the dead
They sit at your table to stave off
food poisoning; they have caught
your infant from the clutches of a fumbling man.
You are poised in every instant
over the fertile graves of millions.
Nothing
will erase your mother's smile, the gate swinging open

as you step off the school bus, the tug in your chest a sea swell
as you swim always towards your first love.
Do not forget the dead.

Coryn.
Mara.
Ife.

ATTRITION

before breaking open

You married a man with teeth and spleen, with all the liver and sinew God grows for the fortunate. You married him, thinking that no man is more than the sum of his parts, nor is this one. On the day you married him, you woke up whistling new ways to harness sun and wind. The altar was a suture bed. The altar was a soft tongue.

The priest said, "Do you take this man?" You said, "I will take him. I will take him apart."

i. lower right, 1ˢᵗ molar

Bowenite serpentine in the basin of your hands on his jaw.

A small bridal tiger carved into the rock. You say,

"Husband, bite the hand that loves you."

The bone chips he spits glisten olive green.

iii. lower left, 3ʳᵈ molar (wisdom tooth)

You say, "My father was a difficult man." He tilts his head back. Your spitwet knuckles work down his throat, grating a threnody on the roof of his mouth.

You use the broken heel of a crucifix to prise the tooth loose.

Leaving the funeral home, he wilts in your arms, spurs of vitreous calcite stabbing his soft palate.

You rinse him off at the standpipe
by the swollen belly-moon of a maticoor night.

ii. upper left, 2nd bicuspid

A stream of talc runs through his hairline, vermillion for the woman he hoped he could become. You tear a pallav over his eyelids, and knot him low to the earth.

Sequins sting his skin.

You say, "You think you're going to die tonight. You're wrong."

Saffron and plasma cling to his shins.

CLINK CLINK

When you were young, you learned to keep out of the bar.
This kept you decent.
You had scrubbed knees, a moon face, two hairplaits like black rope,
thick as pregnant pit vipers with red ribbon tongues.

At nine, you bled.

At twelve, you listened to your nani when she said –
Stand by the Carib fridge and stay still.
Don't look into the bar. Don't smile. Don't move.
Prashant uncle want to see how big you get.

You counted sixteen cold Carib.
A Green Shandy.
Eleven Stag.
The icepick forgotten from the last defrost.
A basin of scotch bonnet, waiting to be pepper sauce.

You drew a smiley face on the condensation.
You were grinding dhal, and there was yellow dust on your legs.
You never forget the shortpants you had on.

In truth, you still don't know any man named Prashant.

All you recall
is a bar fridge reflection, a haze of chest hair, a flash of platinum bera.
A clink, to say you wasn't ugly.
A clink clink, to say you was real nice.

After that day,
you stood outside the bar window, counting everything in sight.

CAMP BURN DOWN

You and me and the fires we used to keep each other alive.
The fire at Camp Balandra.
The fire at Fort George.
The fire at fuck my throat
while my mother's on the phone, and the island's flooding
so everyone's indoors
but you are the skinniest raft
not provided for by the government,
unlawful from here to Tobago
and back.

There are small welts on the backs
of your hands as you braid me
down to the campsite.
This is the camp of Sunday afters,
your father's car radio
melting our eardrums while you move in me.
This is the fort of no retracing, every
place on my body you touch
burned nova,
burned past recognition.
You burn me into an atlas
into a Form One geometry tin
gripped
inside a prefect's handspan,
cock to cock to cheap vaseline,
burning me something new in each fire.

Snow might come to Tunapuna,
and your father would still spill
my guts in front of the market.
There would be hail in the public library,
and your father's pig cutlass
opening my thigh. The weather could vomit itself,

turn the catalogues of gale and gust inside out,
and the biggest damage would be
what I've done to you.

Remember the camp at the edge of the island?

The white stones brining to nothing
as you nerve-ground them between thumb and tongue,
scattering the wet cremations on my forehead.

I bless you, you said, I bless you here.
Nothing touched us except the rest of the world.

THE LECTURE OF DEAD GOLD

When my grandmother died, we
melted the gold she never wore in life.

We unearthed the Priya's and Khan's boxes
like confection houses of the dead,
prising loose bangles and arm-snakes,
shaking out the hutch-hoard of dowries,
taking inventory of a thousand joys.

Wear them for love, Mama says,
sinking thick posts into cartilage.

My brother wears the earrings and kisses his man raw.
He calls it Gethsemane
on the Priority Bus Route after midnight,
sucks olive oil out the red stripe
of Khaled's mouth.

I wear the earrings three evenings before Divali.
They are too heavy, too holy,
an All Souls' slap to the jaw,
dealt slant and sharp like
the first time my grandmother cut my cheek with her love.
The hooks draw blood, digging for Sunday drives,
trawling for breastmilk,
pushing argentum through sore flesh
til memory sings,

'til I quit the graveyard at Freeport,
ears stretched
and bleeding out.

WHAT FIGHTS, STILL

Only,
you don't think love from a woman can do this,
transfix you grinning to the receiver with
your jacket half-shrugged away.

This isn't how you reckon love comes.
A susurration from a mouth still tender with your kisses.

You kiss her like wildfire levels dry bush.
You can't give her less
than the ruination of you.

You left her mouth scorched.
You can hear her lungs work, clear across town.
You can hear her heart working, making music,
setting her rooms to light.
The phone line is dead and you can
hear her dancing.

Her calves are brown and strong.
Her hair tangles when you think of her
and you think of her often.

You work the knots free in the hours between midnight and six;
your fingers singed with lightning and libretti.

Three days from now there will be red stains in her best linen,
an embroidery of bruises over your clavicles,
an aria that unwinds its coda,
thrilling when you swallow,
thrilling
when you remember her in the field,
the aching writhe,
the fluttering bellow.

Your interrogations lace and list,
numbered thick with her.
Nothing in you lacks her colour,
so you call it love.

You call it any name.
You watch it trespass over your barbed wire,
see it steal the horror of that train back home,
the day your father fitted you out,
a man.

You watch her hoard the worst of you,
defenestrate it whole.
Old pottery shards and pellet guns
hurtling to an earth and iron grave.

CROSSDRESSING AT DIVALI NAGAR

The glass bangles are the easiest to steal.

I use spit to force them on you,
knuckling into each one with a soft growl.
You succumb, wrists out,
pink glancing on yellow hitting red,
each one cheap and pure.

My sister's first ohrni comes next.
It's thin like stretched surgical gauze,
spangled like America,
and I smooth it over your cheeks before I kiss
the gaps moths have loved with their teeth.

For sindoor, red lipstick smashed under thumb.
For tika, a rhinestone glued between your eyes.

We giggle like blind chicks gaggling free of the slaughterhouse,
and I scoop cotton candy into your mouth
under the four arms of Mother Lakshmi, my sari and yours
trailing the wooden floorboards of a mehendi booth.
Inside, women and girls are paying for sunbursts,
cloud-spirals, lotus vines looping one good wedlock
after another into their veins.

For adoration, I steal a cone of henna in both your names.

On your knees, under the stage full of dancers,
I trace a lotus onto your back, a broken moon between
the segments of your toes,
a trishula in the furrow of your brow,
its three prongs splitting open when you catch me by the wrist,

your bangles courting the blink and startle of deya light.

FATHERHOOD

is the bruise I only pretend to scrape away on Sunday visits to
Golden Grove;

is the catechism book of the church of my cousin,
his voice in my ear saying
I believe in you, I believe in you,
I believe you won't wreck this;

is the drive back to Quinam with Tracy Chapman coming through deep
like the first woman to save herself
the first law to write herself
the first verse quieting on my mouth like an heirloom punch,
shining purple with value;

is the beach at night when all the puncheon is done in my uncle's house,
is my cousin's hand in mine under every star
is my cousin's hand under my shirt
the realization that Columbus used motions like this to caulk his ships –
steady, firm, taking
everything all at once.

VIVEK CONSIDERS THE NATURE OF SECRETS

Last night, I dreamed Kali was in our kitchen again.
She licked the pots clean with lightning,
scrying yesterday's dhal for black vine weevils.
She weighed turmeric in the wet hollow of her belly, shook
bay leaves loose from the matted beds of her black locks.

Maa, I watched her.
I watched her char those beetles alive and flinching, turmeric-thick
and enflamed.
When she danced, she rattled the floorboards with longing,
crushing skulls beneath her toes in caves of white powder.

Maa, it isn't only her.
Shiva grinned at me going round the Queen's Park Savannah,
pink blossoms braided into his tough-dreads. Krishna
ground his crotch on me during the boat ride you thought was mandir,
learning me fresh prayers. Maa,
I've been anointed
in condom slick and curry powder,
assless briefs and bharatnatyam bells,
stolen mascara and frangipani
plucked from Nani's garden.

Maa, help me say
what I came here to say.

Last night, I whispered to Kali that the boy I most loved
just turned seventeen, redhaired and freckled everyplace
I haven't seen yet but pray towards.

All our gods are raving in me with what I'm scared to call devotion.
At night, Krishna thickens in my ribs, pushing blue-fist first towards
my full sternum of noes.

VIVEK CHOOSES HIS HUSBANDS

Your father said not to take faggots to your bed, so you called them festivals.

Corpus Christi gave his body up between bites of bread,
leavened a Sunday on your tongue so hot
that you chased the burn with olive oil,
sprung from some garden where other men
have fallen to their knees.
You knifed the best sounds of him clean
with eucharist-butter, blessed the back and the sides of his body,
going over catechism scars with tonguepoint,
cock heavy and poised for betrayal.

You splinter the colours of Phagwa in your bed. You let him abeer-bleed
your sheets, consummation morning a slitthroat red,
powder on your lashes, red powder on your nosebridge, joy soft as if you
were sucking that nectar from the cunt of an improbable other.
Small suitors of red
lining the backs of his knees. You cling to the backs of his knees
and let the temple peal bells of bright orgasm over you.

Samhain you found in an Aberystwyth dive bar, and when he asked you
What island does your voice come from, handsome?
You showed him mouth-first, worked glottals over his girth, tasted his
grandfather's name in your soft palate for weeks after,
the ancestry of him roving in your spit,
routing you for fire,
cleaning you for the virgin-kill.

The day you marry Hanukkah is a glock pointed to your father's face.

You tell him
I am the queen
the comeuppance
the hard heretic that nature intended.

ABOUT THE AUTHOR

Shivanee Ramlochan is a Trinidadian poet, arts reporter and book blogger. She reviews Caribbean literature for the *Trinidad and Tobago Guardian*'s Sunday Arts Section, and is the Book Reviews Editor for *Caribbean Beat Magazine*. Shivanee also writes about books for the NGC Bocas Lit Fest, the Anglophone Caribbean's largest literary festival, as well as for Paper Based Bookshop, Trinidad and Tobago's oldest independent Caribbean specialist bookseller. She is the deputy editor of *The Caribbean Review of Books*.